BLUFF YOUR WAY
IN
COMPUTERS

Stan S. Spence
Robert Ainsley
Alexander C. Rae

CENTENNIAL PRESS

ISBN 0-8220-2205-2
U.S. edition © Copyright 1989 by Centennial Press
British edition © Copyright 1988 by The Bluffer's Guides

Printed in U.S.A.

Centennial Press, Box 82087, Lincoln, Nebraska 68501
an imprint of Cliffs Notes, Inc.

COMPUTER BLUFF

It's the easiest thing in the world to bluff people into believing that you're a computer expert. Simply drop all words from your conversation except "the," "and," "initialization," and "configuration," and then fill up the spaces with letters, numbers, and a few jargon words.

The only disadvantage of this method is that when you're dealing with the public, you may begin to notice a strange reaction in your listeners. First, their eyes glaze over; then they suddenly remember an important appointment. On the other hand, if you try this bluff with a real computer expert, he (usually only a "he" is strange enough for this vocation, but a good bluffer doesn't make any rash assumptions) will immediately accept *you* as an expert and respond enthusiastically in exactly the same way. At this point *your* eyes will probably glaze over, shortly before you suddenly remember an important appointment.

Since the point of bluffing is to make yourself more exotic and interesting, this simple form can rarely be recommended, but that doesn't mean it's difficult to bluff in this field. The general public holds computers and computer people in awe, convinced that both are intrinsically intelligent and interesting. At no time should the public ever be given the slightest hint of the truth.

There is actually no activity in which it is easier to be accepted on equal terms with experts—as long as you follow these seven Golden Rules for Computer Bluffers.

Golden Rules for Computer Bluffers

1. The "Today I'm an expert on PC-DOS" ploy.

Always be an "expert" on a different type of computer from that of the person you're talking to. While computers often look the same on the outside, inside the only similarity they have is that they all work on electricity (except for the abacus, of course, which works on gas). One of the main areas of difference is the **operating system** – a delightfully vague concept that no one knows too much about, so there's little chance that anyone will ask you a meaningful question about why it's so important.

Just mention to a UNIX expert that you work only on PC-DOS (or vice versa), and you are suddenly totally and utterly safe. This comment is the computer person's equivalent of saying, "Oh, by the way, I speak Swahili and don't understand a word of English." In fact, there's probably a greater chance of meeting a fluent Swahili/English translator at a party than of finding a computer expert fluent in two operating systems.

If you're surrounded by experts and worried that someone might understand both PC-DOS and UNIX (although computer experts seldom get invited to good parties), make up your own operating system. There are many really obscure formats, usually devised for a computer that sold three models before the company went into bankruptcy, so no one is likely to object that they have never heard of your operating system.

Remember to end the name of your phony operating system with DOS (DOS stands for **Disk Operating System;** whatever you do, don't start talking about loading tapes — that's a dead giveaway that you're really a Commodore VIC-20 owner). Virtually anything ending in DOS will do, but be wary of using the old "DUM-S-DOS." It's unlikely that real computer buffs will get the joke, but you might just be unlucky enough to meet one with a sense of humor.

2. The "Oh, still using that one!" putdown.

Always sneer at every computer or operating system, other than your own. Experts in other operating systems will sneer at *your* operating system, as if they were once experts on it but rejected it as useless, even if it's one that you've made up.

If your opponents admit to having an 8-**bit** machine, claim to have a 16-bit machine. If they have a 16-bit machine, claim to have a 32-bit machine (although if they have a 32-bit, it would be pushing things a little to claim to have a 64-bit machine). Don't worry about the difference between 8-, 16-, and 32-bit machines. Few people in the world could explain what the exact difference really is (something having to do with a bus, which sounds totally ridiculous), so you can just assume that a 16-bit is twice as good as an 8-bit, and so forth.

3. The "I wouldn't dirty my hands" opening.

Never admit to using a computer for any practical purpose. Never mention using a **spreadsheet, database,** or, worst of all, a **word processor.** The real com-

5

puter bluffer should have a computer only for some peculiarly esoteric purpose having to do with **programming.** To admit that you gained some commercial advantage from your computer is like an avant-garde poet admitting to writing greeting-card verses.

4. The "It needs a little tweaking" gambit.

Never admit to using a commercial program. If you're forced to admit that you use something, say you run a PD program (see **Public Domain**), but you wouldn't recommend that everyone use it because it takes a little **tweaking** to get it to run.

Tweaking is a technical term that means taking someone else's program, usually written for a different computer, and improving it or adapting it to work on your machine. (It's like those people who devote their lives to taking the engine out of a Volkswagen and replacing it with one from a Lear Jet. However, tweaking isn't as much fun and usually has less chance of success.)

Ninety-nine times out of a hundred you will be perfectly safe with this routine. Anyone with any pretensions to being a computer buff has a houseful of PD programs that they can't get to work – programs bought on the recommendation of a friend who mentioned that "all it needs is a little tweaking." They will never attempt to use the nonexistent program that you've recommended, although they might recommend it to someone else. If you're really lucky, you could one day find your spurious program being recommended to you – although "it might need a little tweaking." If this happens, you can regard yourself as a master bluffer.

If you have to quote a name, remember that all PD

programs have names made up of words with the vowels missing, like SPRDSHT, or are just a random selection of letters (see **TLA**). Pretend to have gotten it from **PC-SIG** or **Exec-PC** or to have downloaded it from a bulletin board.

5. The "And now for my next trick" trick.

Always be on the point of buying a new, far more powerful computer. It should be a "fifth generation portable 32-bit machine" with "true multitasking" that can handle Mandelbrot equations and perform open heart surgery at the same time. If anyone dares to admit that they haven't heard of it, just say that Apple still has it under wraps but that it was being whispered about at COMDEX. No one will disbelieve that.

6. The "In your day they loaded programs with tape recorders" gambit.

It's a general rule throughout the computer industry that you should be young. Very young. There's no point in bragging at age 25 that you can program in Pascal. Within minutes you will be confronted by a nine-year-old who has been programming in **assembler** for the last two years. It's simpler to keep dying your hair and never admit to remembering a time when there wasn't a right wing in the Republican party.

In the same vein, remember that the computer industry is one of the few spheres of activity where experience is totally useless. Even as a new computer is launched on the market, the company's **R and D** (Research and Development) team has already developed one with twice the capacity at half the

7

size—which is, of course, totally incompatible with the existing model.

Do not be impressed by stories of years of computer experience. Anything learned ten minutes ago is liable to be out of date. Anything learned ten years ago is as useful as hunting a saber-toothed tiger with a flint-tipped spear.

7. Become a master of the TLA.

By far, the most important concept you have to grasp to be a successful computer bluffer is how to use the **TLA**—the only piece of computer technology that is common in every form of computer from the 32k game machines to the massive mainframes. There is no area of computing that does not use the TLA extensively, and knowledge of how to use it properly can confer immediate status on its user. The TLA, of course, stands for the **Three Letter Abbreviation.**

How the TLA was invented is lost in the mists of antiquity. Why three letters should be chosen is a total mystery. It has been suggested that "three" was picked by early computer aces because of the well-known fact that computers can count only up to two (see **Binary**), and this disability was proof that their human operators were still superior.

A great deal of ingenuity has gone into creating the most unlikely TLAs. The original idea was that the letters should be the initials of real words, but this intent is of only passing interest to the computer buff. People quite happily use TLAs for many years without the slightest idea of what they really mean. For instance, people use TLAs such as **CRT** or **VDT** every day without knowing that they mean **Cathode Ray**

Tube and **Video Display Terminal** – both referring, of course, to the computer's screen.

Never think the TLA makes for easier conversation. Try saying "CRT" and then "screen," and decide which one you think is easier to utter. The real reason for the TLA is

(1) to cause confusion
(2) to be intentionally obscure
(3) to allow the user to feel smug, much as lawyers use Latin

Use the TLA mercilessly. The only areas to avoid are ones that are so well known that everyone thinks they know what they mean (CIA, IRS, FBI, etc.). Once you're sure that you're not competing with a real TLA, the rest of the alphabet is yours to play with (you would need a computer to work out the number of possibilities).

So never again say three words when three letters will do. A good computer bluffer will take the NNB (Number Nine Bus) to his POE (Place of Employment) after a good breakfast of KRB (Kellogg's Raisin Bran).

Computers and the Public

Life is much easier if you are dealing with a member of the public. The only facts known by the average person about computers are

(1) They're screwed up when your paycheck/gas bill/income tax is not right.
(2) They allow you to shoot down an infinite number of green nasties from outer space and save civilization as we know it.

(3) They allow you to phone the Pentagon and read "top secret" files listing all the important details of our national defense before they're printed in the *New York Times*.

The major misconception that the public seems to have is that computers do interesting things. This is totally and utterly wrong. Computers are really best at doing a lot of very boring things very quickly. But don't admit this to anyone who hasn't realized it.

The average person has absolutely no idea what you actually do with a computer. The art of true computer bluffing is to convince the layman that you're doing something really significant with it, without ever letting slip what it is. Since genuine computer experts spend a lot of time doing the same thing, there's no chance you'll be labeled a fraud.

Microchips with Everything

It's true to say that **microchips** are taking over our lives. Everyone who has turned on a washing machine, read the time from a digital watch, or drunk coffee out of one of those mugs that play "Happy Birthday to You" every time you pick up the miserable thing has first-hand experience with microchips.

These mundane uses do not make microchips any more understandable to the man-in-the-street. If anything, it just confuses him further when he tries to figure out why multinational companies would invest millions of dollars on mainframe computers that play "Happy Birthday to You" very loudly when you pick them up.

Use of the Manual

While computer and software manufacturers have made great advances in making computers and programs more user-friendly (they now have error messages like "Sorry! Fatal System Error!"), the vast majority of people over the age of 30 still regard computers as mysterious, temperamental things that need instinctive and sensitive handling. If they ever found out that all you need is a logical mind and two typing fingers to use virtually any piece of software, many thousands of bluffers would be unceremoniously dumped on the unemployment scrap heap. Or forced to get a real job.

Only one thing stands between us and this terrible predicament – the **software manual.** Reading the average software manual makes you realize that the computer industry has been infiltrated at the highest levels by some of the top bluffers in the country.

Everyone knows the First Law of Microprocessing: **If all else fails, read the manual** or, sometimes, **RT*M.** A true bluffer would never make such an irresponsible statement because this document is a vital element in a bluff that has kept the general public out of computers for years.

If you're ever faced with the unthinkable – actually having to get a piece of software to work – tackle it by playing around with the program and finding out by trial and error how it works. Once you've mastered the program, you can go to the manual and figure out what it actually means. This might take some time, so accept no dinner invitations for the next two years.

If anyone else needs to use the software, insist that they start by reading the manual from cover to cover.

Say something like "You'll find the appendix on BIOS calls invaluable." It doesn't matter if there aren't any appendices. They won't get that far. They'll still be plowing their way through helpful pieces of information like "The syntax for this command is EDIT [FROM] >filename> [[TO] <filename>] [WITH <filename>] [VER <filename>][OPT <option>]" or maybe "Designated drive: ambiguous filename: argument." If they believe you've understood this and gone on to run the program, your reputation will be assured forever.

Helpful Error Messages

As well as being armed with a good thick manual, you should have a plentiful supply of **error messages** – helpful little phrases that appear on the screen to announce that something has gone awry and you've just lost all your work for the last month.

There's a game played by computer programmers to see who can produce the longest and most obscure error message in the world. One strong contender that appeared on a mainframe computer was the message, "VME ERROR 3702 Hierarchic name syntax invalid taking into account starting points defined by initial context." That's a real one. Most programs are remembered not for their power of user-friendliness but for the originality and creativity of their error messages. One manufacturer at least has the sense of humor to refer to them as **guru messages.**

Once you realize it's all a game, you can face "Unexpected diagnostic verification violation" flashing on your screen with absolute calm. Where error messages come in really useful is when you reach that point when someone asks you to do something on the computer and *you don't know how to do it.* A normal person would stupidly blurt out something like "I don't know how to do that." But the bluffer just smiles quietly, confidently presses a few significant-looking keys, stares at the screen with a worried expression, and when nothing happens, murmurs, "Oh boy. Looks like we've got severe mantissa buffering overload in the high addresses."

Strictly speaking, that doesn't mean anything. But strangely enough, no one has ever been known to ask what it does mean. If you're a really enthusiastic bluffer, you might experiment until you find a method of consistently producing a real error message (it's remarkably easy). Then let the other person decide whether you should go on once you have been warned that there is an "Untrapped illegal stack deficiency in 720."

Here are three useful error messages you can use, with a short explanation of what they mean.

"Severe retrieval format corruption" (nothing)
"Nonrecoverable global drivespec mixing in 4070" (nothing)
"Terminal high byte consolidation violation" (nothing)

Educating the Public

Experienced bluffers soon realize that there's more to life than keeping the public in a state of ignorance. Aside from anything else, such a state can quickly become total paranoia about everyone and everything connected with computers—which could result in your being shunned by everyone except politicians looking for your vote and evangelists looking for your money.

So it's important that you try to explain to the average person the seemingly contradictory facts that

(1) Computers are extremely complex.
(2) Anyone can quickly learn how they work – assuming that they are reasonably intelligent (their IQ measures 140 on a bad day).

Since no one will ever admit to being stupid, you'll be sure of a rapt and grateful audience, particularly if you begin to detail to what extent computers already govern our lives. You will, in fact, become something of a hero in the public's eyes. Remember, your mission is to explain. The fact that people probably won't understand one word in ten doesn't matter. That's their fault, not yours.

Computers and Numbers

People mistakenly believe that computers have a lot to do with numbers, which is totally inaccurate. In fact, a large number of bluffers have gone into computers because there's no area in which it's easier to hide a complete inability to count, except perhaps mathematics.

You should realize that computer figures don't actually mean anything because

(1) Nearly all the numbers you use are actually names for really obscure things.
(2) There are so many really obscure things with numbers instead of names that whatever number you happen to quote will probably be accurate.

Above all, remember that you will never be asked

to add or subtract them, or anything difficult like that.

If you really want to do any computations with numbers, buy yourself a pocket calculator. They're far easier to use, don't stop working unexpectedly as often, and are usually more accurate than computers. One good way to annoy real computer people is to secretly use your pocket calculator to work out the square root of 43, accurate to 27 significant points, and then talk in a loud voice about how you got your computer to do it. But leave the room before they torture you to find out how you did it. Note that they will never ask why you want the square root of 43, accurate to 27 points. This information comes under the heading of an "interesting" (useless) thing you can get your computer to do.

The only really important numbers you have to remember are the ones in your computer's name. All computers have a number somewhere in their title, which may or may not mean something. If you have invented a computer for yourself, always add a number. The Doppleganger ZQ768, for instance, would do just fine. To make it really authentic, always choose a number that can be divided by **256**, the computer's mystical number.

Binary

The main thing you need to remember about computers and numbers is that computers can count only up to one (starting at zero, of course). These numbers are called **binary** numbers and are of no practical use to anyone using a computer—which does not stop anyone who purports to know anything about computers from explaining binary in detail at the drop of

15

a floppy disk. There are computer magazines that will insist on filling a page on binary in an article telling you how to plug your computer into the wall socket.

Your primary purpose in discussing binary is to confuse your listeners so much that they won't see the gaping holes in your reasoning in later discussions. You should therefore start any conversation with the computer illiterate with a lengthy discussion of binary.

Hex

If your listeners look as if they are perhaps beginning to grasp the idea of binary, immediately slip into a lecture on hex numbers without any explanation. **Hexadecimal** numbers (or **hex** as it's known to its friends) refers to the system whereby a computer, instead of counting up to one, counts up to 16. (Please note that no matter how clever computers are supposed to be, they never seem to have caught on to the fact that everyone else counts up to 10.)

Since there aren't 16 single digits available, you have to use letters as numbers in hex (0B, for example, in hex represents 11, and 3F in hex is 63. So remember when you quote a hex figure that it will always have two digits, one or both of which could be a letter between *A* and *F*. The only one worth memorizing is that 100 in hex is really 256 — the computer's mystical number. But, of course, since hex numbers have only two digits, you have to start at nothing again.

If at any time others question any figure you mention, just shake your head sadly and point out that you were working in hex. Then giggle quietly to yourself as they try to convert all your numbers into decimal without counting on their fingers.

The major advantage of counting in hex, however, is that on your 40th birthday you can truthfully tell the world you are 28.

ASCII

Should a particularly bright listener show even the slightest potential to grasp the idea of hex quickly, move on to the fact that computers are convinced that letters are numbers. The secret is hidden in the snappily titled **American Standard Code for Information Interchange**—ASCII, pronounced *Ass-key*.

As codes go, this one is childishly easy to break. It turns out that even so-called word processors can't remember letters, so they turn all letters into numbers, which they can remember, but only one and zero if they're working in binary. But not if they're working in hex, when they turn letters into numbers and letters, of course.

The idea is that if you have a file translated into this ASCII code, it can be read by virtually any computer. What they don't tell you is that if you have an ASCII file on an 8″ disk, it's hard to shove it into a 3½″ disk drive.

WHICH COMPUTER?

The first thing you have to decide is which computer you'll be an expert on. There are computers of every size and description, but you still have to be careful to pick one that suits your image. Here's a rundown on the main types.

Mainframes

Mainframes are the big, impressive computers that add K-Mart's telephone bill to yours. They look like everyone's idea of what computers should look like. They fill several air-conditioned rooms. It is sad that there seem to be no computers like the ones in movies—the ones with 15,000 red lights that flash on and off constantly and make strange buzzing noises. This state of affairs is largely due to the fact that no one has yet thought up any purpose for the 15,000 flashing lights and that no one could afford the electric bill anyway.

These days the computer that used to fill two rooms can be contained in something about the size of a folded *New York Times* Sunday edition. Miniaturization has now probably reached its limit. In fact, work has had to stop on the latest Japanese 32k game machines, since the designer put the prototype down somewhere and can't find it again. It can therefore be seen that the computers that still fill two rooms are what those in the computer world call "pretty big."

Today the major area of development in mainframes is thinking up new names for the numbers of calculations a computer can do in a **nanosecond** (in technical terms, a nanosecond is a "really short time"). They quickly outstripped mere millions, billions, and trillions. Zillion still comes in useful for the smaller machines, but the really big ones nowadays have to talk in frillions and squillions of calculations per nanosecond. Note that no one ever asks who it is that has this number of calculations to do. And why they want them done so quickly. Maybe it's because it might have something to do with the national debt and we don't really want to know about it.

A great deal of time is given to thinking up names for the amount of **memory** one of these computers has. When they discovered that the faithful old **gigabyte** (one thousand megabytes) wasn't enough, they had to rush and invent the **terabyte** (one thousand gigabytes). To give you some idea how big a terabyte is, it could probably contain all the information from all the Rolodexes in the world (including China). Unfortunately, any computer with a terabyte of memory would fill a couple of air-conditioned rooms the size of Cleveland, but they're working on that. If you intend to pass yourself off as a mainframe expert, you can make up your own memory size for your computer, although it's best to avoid a "beer and byte."

Before you rush off to become a mainframe expert, you have to take into consideration one small problem. If computers are good at doing a lot of boring things quickly, mainframes are *really* good at doing an *un-*

imaginable number of *very* boring things *very* quickly. They cost so much that only insurance companies, banks, and television evangelists can afford them. It's hard to be in the "in crowd" while claiming to be in charge of computing Social Security payments for the whole state of West Virginia.

There are only one or two areas of mainframe computing that could be regarded as even vaguely romantic. The first area is **AI** (**Artificial Intelligence** not Artificial Insemination – don't try to impress a farmer by saying you're in AI, or he'll ask you to do things that would turn your hair gray). Originally, AI was the theory that a computer could be developed that would effectively mimic human intelligence and develop its own identity and awareness. Why anyone would want to build a computer that would probably demand overtime pay for work in excess of eight hours isn't known. The general belief is that the idea originated with computer programmers desperate to have someone to talk to who wouldn't find them boring. Nonetheless, work began on this concept largely because

(1) Government coughed up huge amounts of money for research.
(2) It employed all sorts of philosophers, psychologists, mathematicians, and linguists who were otherwise unemployable.
(3) There was always the chance that an AI machine could predict the winner of the next Super Bowl.

The second possibly romantic area is the military, which seemingly has World War III already on disk. The computers will launch the missiles, aim the guns, plan the strategy, polish the boots, and play the bugle first thing in the morning. All that's needed is a general bright enough to understand the manual.

Terminals

The next stage down from having a mainframe to play with is having a **terminal** (a screen and keyboard which are connected to a mainframe – nothing to do with a serious illness). This piece of property can give you a real feeling of power, knowing that you are tying up part of a multimillion-dollar computer as you type out a letter to your mother using two fingers.

Apart from this, the terminals are not much fun. You can get all the financial software to buy and sell shares at the stock exchange, and that kind of thing, but they are woefully short of good adventure games, and virtually none have anywhere to attach a joystick or a mouse.

The best examples of the use of these machines are the systems they have for laying out the pages in the new "colored" newspapers like *USA Today*. Some newspapers have now gone to the length of putting everything, including the air conditioning, in the same computer – to such an extent that when anyone turns on the central cooling system, the computer misspells every name on the front page. This result is, of course, a real technological advance. Until now, it has taken up to ten reporters and four editors to misspell every name on the front page.

Micros/Minis/Personal Computers

This is where you came in. That Commodore 64 collecting dust in the closet makes you a **micro** user. Sadly, this description covers about 95 percent of the population, so don't make too much of it.

However, you can't ignore the fact that **microcomputers** have provided the computer world with its longest standing and most contentious controversy. Wherever you find two or three computer buffs gathered together, it won't be long before the fateful question is asked, "Do you spell it *disc* or *disk?*"

Disks (or discs) are strange creatures. Despite the name, they are never round, although they can be square with a round hole in the middle. They can vary in shape from dinky little flat plastic things to massive boxes. Anything that is not a massive box is called a **floppy disk** despite the fact that they aren't floppy, and the big boxes are called **hard disks** despite the fact they are usually square or rectangular.

Floppies come in the sort of standard sizes you would expect in a high-tech, modern industry: 3″, 3½″, 5¼″, and 8″. This state of affairs is all part of the computer industry's goal of achieving one standard of incompatibility. You may be able to run the same software on all computers, but you'll never know because the disk won't fit in the disk drive you own.

To complicate it further, some floppy disks can be used on only one side and others can be used on both. The two-sided ones are sometimes referred to as **flippy-floppies.** From this example, make up your own. For example, corrupted disks that lose part of their data could be "sloppy-floppies" or even "jippy-flippies." Be careful though not to get ridiculous.

Laptop or Portable Computers

Laptops are the wave of the future

- not because they allow computer designers to show off how well they can miniaturize equipment
- not because they allow you to take your work with you anywhere from the top of a mountain to the beach ("You must be joking," you can tell anyone who suggests it)
- but because you can use them on a plane

It is at this point that you discover the real ignorance of the public about computers. People don't interrupt your work to ask questions about baud rates or operating systems. All they want to ask is the basic question "What are you doing?" To anyone with half a brain, the answer is obvious. There is only one thing you can be doing using a computer on a plane – you're showing off.

Laptops will be the major growth area in computers as more and more people feel the need to show off in planes. It certainly makes keeping your Rolodex up to date look pretty mundane.

COMPUTER USER TYPES

Just as the Japanese always look alike to the Occidental, computer people can all look alike to an inexperienced bluffer. However, with a little practice you should be able to tell them apart and make use of this information. If you discover that you are mixing with one group, be an expert on a different group.

Here is a short rundown of the major groups with "telltale signs" that will allow you to pick out these people immediately.

Programmers

There are two types of people who write **programs:**

(1) programmers
(2) software writers

Programmers write boring business financial programs for companies, are all smart, and have lots of money. They hate their jobs.

Software writers write at home for commercial release. They wear T-shirts and John Lennon glasses and have long hair and beer bellies (both men and women). They spend all of their money on beer and floppy disks. They love their jobs.

Neither type ever talks about the programs they are currently writing, so it's easy to pass yourself off as one.

Telltale signs. Strange sense of humor – they laugh at nothing except non sequiturs because misuse of logic reminds them of the programs they write. They use **k** to mean *thousand,* as in "I hear they're offering him 25k plus a company car."

When to pretend to be a software writer. When in the company of software writers, who will buy you lots of beer.

Mistakes to avoid in conversation. Asking what program they're currently working on.

I've-Computerized-My-Business Types

These people have bought one or two cheap computers in the vague hope that they will "streamline things," "get ahead," and "save money in the long run." They end up having to pay for expensive maintenance contracts in case things go wrong; they send their staff on costly computer training courses every month at several hundred dollars per person per day; and they get several months behind as they learn to use their computers. Their only benefit is that they can now blame every mistake on "computer error" to credulous customers.

Never believe any nonsense they tell you about the "paperless office," the idea that all your paperwork can be stored on disk instead of paper. Point out that using a micro necessitates

- boxes and boxes of continuous paper piled next to the printer

- manuals for the software you use
- books telling you how to actually use the software because the manual is a literal translation from the Japanese
- more wastepaper baskets for the printing, which prints half off the page the first time you do 2000 customer letters
- boxes of disks
- boxes of backup disks for emergency copies of the original disks
- printouts of all the documents which have been put on disk anyway

Telltale signs. Inky fingers from having changed the printer ribbon four times during their print run of 2000 customer letters. Haggard, tired expression. Dogged belief that it'll all come out right in the end. Irrational trust in new technology.

When to pretend to be a computerized business-person. When trying to convince your customers that the wrong invoice you sent was "computer error."

Mistakes to avoid in conversation. "Tell me, how do you handle your accounts?"

Dedicated Word Processors

Everyone knows the one about the infinite number of monkeys with an infinite number of typewriters producing the entire works of Shakespeare in an infinite amount of time. Since the invention of the **word processor,** the job can be done much more quickly. And it would seem there are already a large number of monkeys started on the mammoth task – disguised as a group of people called **dedicated word processors.**

These souls are a strange breed, largely because they may not even know that they own a computer. Many seem to spend their lives thinking a word processor is the machine they're working with, not the **program** that they're running on the computer. Many would be surprised to discover that their word processor can count. The most daring are inclined to buy adventure games, and if they get them to work, they consider themselves to be hackers.

They are often married women with growing children who have bought a computer to write books for *Harlequin Romances* rather than let their brains atrophy. Or retired colonels who live under the strange delusion that people will be interested in finding out what they did during the war and who also end up writing for *Harlequin Romances* using a female pen name. There's no use trying to bluff these people with technical terms. They know none and are completely unperturbed if you point out this fact to them. To this bunch, getting technical means finding out how to set tabs on a page.

Yet, without fail, they'll be able to tell you how it's possible to use the SEARCH/REPLACE command to change, with a single stroke, every occurrence of the name *Smith* in a 100,000 word novel to the name *Jones.* They never give you a solid reason why you should want to do this—but rest assured that your life will be much poorer if you can't.

The real danger is that dedicated word processors will use the pretext of talking about computers to tell you every detail of the plot development in their four-volume, blockbuster novel about passion and intrigue among the passengers on the Chicago-Denver Amtrak run.

Telltale signs. Several publishers' rejection slips sticking out of every pocket.

When to pretend to be a dedicated word processor. Only when you meet an attractive member of the opposite sex who has some literary pretensions – combining the attractions of knowledge of computers with a creative streak.

Mistakes to avoid in conversation. Saying, "What is it you write about?"

Hackers

Hacking sounds as if it should be the most romantic pastime for computer aces. It isn't.

There are two kinds of **hacker:**

(1) One uses a **modem** to hack into the Pentagon's communications system to gain access to the nation's defense secrets. This avocation can be quite exciting, especially during the trial.

(2) The other spends years of his life pouring through meaningless **machine code** (screen after screen of numbers with a few letters thrown in) to look for **pokes.** It is obvious that these are lonely people, lacking in social graces, since they believe it's possible to talk about *pokes* in polite society and get away with it.

Pokes (not to be confused with peeks) are highly obscure jumbles of numbers and letters which you can type into your computer to allow you to do important things, like getting infinite lives while playing *Space Invaders* (or as one computer magazine stated about a bouncing-ball game, "This poke means you won't lose your balls even if you deserve to.").

Whether you consider this a worthwhile result after years of study and research is up to you. The more serious hackers do interesting things like "accessing ROM directly," but whether this makes them better people or not is never really explained.

Hackers are sometimes referred to as **computer nerds** and are characterized by thick Coke-bottle-lens glasses and a pocket protector with 19 pens in it and are usually carrying a 963-page, dog-eared book called *The Advanced Manual for MS-DOS Users*. A hacker has been defined as someone who knows 726 ways of making love but doesn't know any girls.

Certain enlightened souls have discovered a standard utility available on nearly every computer. This utility allows you to look at machine code and make minor changes to programs. These intrepid hackers ignore all the difficult parts (the code) and home in on the **prompts,** which can be simply changed. The real bluffers merely change the program credits, replacing the programmer's or company's name with their own. They can then look suitably modest when someone notices that they are credited with having written an industry-standard spreadsheet like *Lotus 1-2-3.* Since such "adjustments" are highly illegal, they must check very carefully to be sure they're not showing the software to someone from the FBI.

Telltale signs. An ability to say, "I've got a great poke for *Marble Madness*" without seeing anything funny in it.

29

Mistakes to avoid in conversation. Talking about hacking.

When to be a bluffing hacker. Anytime you can get away with it.

PD Enthusiasts

You can tell what cheapskates **PD** enthusiasts are by the fact that they don't even bother to acquire a full three letter abbreviation. *PD* stands for **Public Domain**—a quixotic idea that programs should not be bought and sold in a sordid, moneygrubbing way but should be given away instead.

Clubs are set up to distribute PD software. They give away all these programs completely free—except for the cost of membership, a disk, and of course, a small handling charge and postage and packaging—and then there's sales tax, a small service charge, and . . . (In fact, there's only one club that still holds to the true standards of PD, and that's the club that any PD enthusiast you meet happens to belong to.)

PD clubs (also known as **user groups**) draw their software from a number of areas. Some people offer their programs from a real belief in the principles of PD—or in other words, they have a truly useful program but don't have the money to promote it properly. Rather than sell it to a software publisher, they unselfishly give it away in the hope of making considerably more money.

The way these people make their money is by selling you a manual. Since it should be possible to run any *good* software without opening the manual (ask

any computer journalist), the programmers go to a lot of trouble to make sure that their programs cannot be run without the most obscure instructions possible. By the time they've thought up all the most unlikely key-presses, you feel less like you're running a program and more like you're playing a Chopin polonaise.

A second source of software is the program that's been touted as a sure-fire commercial success but hasn't yet found a software publisher to promote it. Rather than see hours of work go down the drain, the creator offers it to other PD enthusiasts in the hope that someone might find it useful and send the author a few dollars in appreciation of his efforts. This optimistic outlook is known as the **shareware** concept. You may have thought some of the commercial programs were lemons, but shareware puts everything in perspective.

The last and major source of software is from the hacker who believes he has done something "interesting" with his computer. These program gems make up 95 percent of PD software and usually involve getting a totally obscure computer to run software that no one has ever heard of. If the hacker could locate the one other person in the free world who has that particular computer and who wants to run that particular software, he might have one buyer; but since that's never happened, it's difficult to be sure. Worse still, when the hacker comes up with a *better* way to run the obscure software on his obscure computer, he will send in an *upgrade* which the PD club will put on its lists as a completely different program. You can thus spend several months buying 27 versions of the same program and still not understand what it does.

Telltale signs. A large number of programs that just need a little tweaking to get them to work.

Mistakes to avoid when talking to a PD enthusiast. Asking what PD software is worth buying.

When to be a bluffing PD enthusiast. At the point of being caught using a program that you obviously haven't written yourself.

Bulletin Board Freaks (BBFs)

Bulletin Board Freaks are not people who derive a great deal of pleasure from reading the ads that people place in supermarkets. That is far too interesting a pastime for the real bulletin board freak—the **BBF.**

Instead, these driven souls spend the whole of their waking lives thinking about communicating with another computer over telephone lines using a **modem.** A modem is a very clever, useful device which attaches your computer to your telephone and allows you to send long streams of text (more numbers with a few letters thrown in) over the telephone line using a high-pitched screaming sound—much like a cat with its tail trapped in a door.

To the unwary, this activity can sound really exciting. It means you are able to communicate with anyone who owns a modem (and a telephone) anywhere in the world. That's fine until you think who, in this particular world, would you want to communicate with.

There is a chance that once you know even one person with a modem, it's unlikely that you would want to communicate with another one. While the advantage of this system is that you can send long streams of text by using the modem, it should be pointed out that receiving that long stream of text from a BBF can be dangerous to your health. People have been known to die of boredom just looking out the window when a BBF was passing their house.

Bulletin boards, or **BBSs (Bulletin Board Systems)** as they are known in the TLA vernacular, are a network of thousands of computers set up to serve as **mailboxes, message centers,** and **datafile repositories** by other BBFs whose biggest thrill in life is listening to their telephones ring. Here BBFs gather to exchange ideas, views, and witty repartee. Since the only things that computer BBFs think about are computers, the bulletin boards are filled with questions about how to solve problems using a certain modem with a certain computer in order to contact more bulletin boards. There are also specialist bulletin boards that allow BBFs with specialized interests to communicate with like-minded people. These usually cover things like ham radio (another mysterious subject to the layman), the propagation of various exotic forms of plant life, strange religious groups, and the more unseemly forms of pornography.

Sooner or later you will meet someone who drones on about how he heard that Isaac Asimov sends the manuscripts of his novels via a satellite to his publishers, who can then typeset directly. Never be impressed by this tale, and point out that even if it were so

(1) No one except Isaac Asimov could afford to rent satellites.
(2) If you send your novel by normal phone lines, it takes several hours ("better your phone bill than mine").

(3) A slicker solution would be to send the manuscript by a data transfer system so accurate it needs no protocol, is cheap (you can send 2k for a quarter), requires no logging-on time, needs no complicated passwords to use, and can reach 100 percent of computer users in the world—it's called the U.S. Postal Service (although referred to by computer users as U.S. Snail).

As with any form of "communications," zealous devotees create jargon and indecipherable technical terms so that any real communication quickly becomes impossible. Conversations in the flesh or through a modem with a BBF consist of a constant flow of references to **baud rates, protocols,** and **handshaking.** The only people more obscure in conversation are CB enthusiasts and radio hams.

Probably the most exciting moment in a a BBF's life is when he **logs on** to a bulletin board with a multiuser capability at the same time as another BBF and has **direct contact** (as one types the words on his keyboard they appear on the other's screen). You can accomplish the same thing even if you don't have a modem. It's called "talking on the telephone."

Luckily enough, BBFs are inclined to want to do their thing in the middle of the night (when the telephone rates are cheapest), so they're often too tired to speak during the day.

Telltale signs. A desire to talk about baud rates.

Mistakes to avoid in conversation. If the BBF mentions Kermit, do not start discussing the Muppets. Kermit is a **protocol** (a method of allowing two computers to talk to each other). The *major* mistake you could make in conversation with a BBF, however, is saying "Hello."

When to be a bluffing BBF. The only time you should try to pretend to be a BBF is when you meet a real hacker.

Game Players

Game Players are people who wear T-shirts and jeans and sit inside on balmy summer evenings in their bedrooms playing adventure games or zapping aliens. They have an encyclopedic knowledge of every screen of every game they have ever played. They get into vehement arguments with other game players about whether the most difficult screen in *Arkanoids* is the fifth or the sixth and whether *Ultima III* is overrated or not.

There are two types of game players:

(1) Ostensibly normal people with responsible jobs who become game players only in the evenings and are ashamed to tell anyone of their inclinations (closet *PacMan* freaks).

(2) Pimple-faced adolescent boys whose bedrooms are full of games and game magazines, to which they write hopelessly ungrammatical and badly spelled letters consisting entirely of the words *rad, dude,* and *warez* (pronounced *wares*), with an occasional *wow* or *great* thrown in, and sign themselves *Mr.,* thinking this will convince somebody.

Telltale signs. A trembling of the thumb while talking to you as they subconsciously work the joystick on level six of *Arkanoids*. B Dalton bags with dozens of new games in them. Baseball caps. Abnormally high use of the words *rad, dude,* and *warez*. Pimples.

When to pretend to be a game player. When you need to establish good relations with adolescents.

Mistakes to avoid in conversation. Talking about high scores.

COMPUTERS IN THE WORLD

Computers are everywhere – although some of their uses are obviously more impressive than others. It is therefore vital for you to choose at an early stage where you want your interest in computers to lie.

Computers in the Office

The office is the most obvious place where a computer might be useful, and it's therefore a place where you should tread warily. This is not to say that there isn't a niche for someone who is prepared to put just a little effort into carving out a highly paid career by means of computer bluffing. Everything depends on finding yourself the right boss. The ideal are those in their 50s who feel that computers are a "good idea" that will make the company "more efficient" but still have only the vaguest idea of what the things do.

Better still, you might find one of that rare breed who takes pride in "knowing nothing about computers." There are still people in positions of authority who blithely announce that they don't understand the first thing about computers in the same sort of way that they would tell you that there is definitely no mental illness in their families. In fact, to them, an ability to understand computers is a definite sign of a warped mind. If you find one of these people, hang in there – you can go far in a company like this.

The best situation is to join the company just after it has spent thousands of dollars on one of those specialized software packages that never works. If you think that's unlikely, remember that until someone discovers *how* the program works (usually about two months after purchase) these packages *don't* work. Someone has to take the blame for having spent thousands of dollars on a product that's useless, so there's usually a vacancy for a **systems manager** about six weeks after the software is installed.

Whatever you do, don't rush and get the software working. That would spoil all the fun and would mean that the boss has nothing to moan about at the country club on Sunday afternoons. You must quickly concede that it just won't work "in its present form." Then after a suitable pause (to build up the tension), reluctantly admit that "with a little tweaking" you *might* be able to get it to work.

Naturally, you don't actually do anything to the program, but if the program suddenly starts working in some form or other, and they believe it was your know-how that got it to work, and they think you are the only person in the world who really knows how it works now, you are suddenly indispensable.

Computers in Schools

Computers are now beginning to creep into the classroom, where they usually perform the useful function of keeping dust off the table they are sitting on.

If each child had full time use of his or her own computer, using the right software, the computer would completely revolutionize education. As a useful first step towards this utopian idea, the powers that be insist that every school should have at least one Apple computer (two, if there are more than 3000 students).

Naturally, this computer gets used mainly for tasks with the highest priority—for the principal's word processing and to allow one of the teachers to play adventure games after four o'clock. Occasionally it's even used for educational purposes—in this case, teaching children that when they get a math problem wrong, a little man shakes his head and makes a noise that sounds something like *Oh-oh*.

Whatever you do, don't get involved with anything to do with computers in schools. There's absolutely no money in it, and without fail, all the kids will know more about computers than you do.

Computers in the Home

There are only two real reasons for having a computer in the home:

(1) as a word processor to write *Bluff Your Way in Computers* on
(2) to play games

Since *Bluff Your Way in Computers* has already been written and no bluffer would ever admit to playing games, it takes a little bit of imagination to decide why computers in the home are a good idea.

Educational Software

One of the bright areas of development is **educa-**

tional software for the home – a boom industry. This sector depends totally on the fact that parents need to convince themselves they haven't bought Johnny a computer just so he can zap little green men from the planet Zud. So the parents will cough up for a succession of rather unlikely programs with tantalizing titles like *Advanced Calculus Can Be Fun* – absolute proof that for some reason the "truth-in-advertising" laws do not apply to software.

Although it can't really be proved, the majority of these educational programs are probably little more than a plausible-looking opening screen. Virtually no one will ever run these programs through to see if they do what they are supposed to do (especially the children that they were intended for).

Home educational software is therefore the easiest field of programming for the bluffer. You could quickly learn enough BASIC to whip up an opening screen and four pages of really dreary questions (about two more pages than are really required). Your only worry is that some overzealous magazine reviewer with a degree in mathematics and a tendency towards masochism may get hold of a copy of your *Barney Bear's Quadratic Equation Game* and run it all the way through. Luckily, many of these people can be easily bribed.

The best educational software programs usually involve dull little math problems or complicated words to spell. There is always a little animated figure that jumps up and down if you get it right or shakes his head and makes the *Oh-oh* noise if you get it wrong. The person who comes up with the hardware to allow the computer to give little Johnny a minor electric shock if he gets it wrong will probably retire early and rich.

Home Finance Packages

Probably the most unlikely thing that people do with a personal computer is to keep track of their home finances. However, these budding Rockefellers don't realize how impractical this endeavor is – until they've invested $99 on a program in the belief that it will save them money.

Usually these packages feature the names of well-known financial experts, thus giving you the impression that using their programs will allow you to become an expert as well. Nothing could be further from the truth.

Again, these programs are pretty easy to write. As the people who buy this sort of program are the types who always read the manual, they'll probably be happy if the screens they see there are impressive, no matter how the program actually functions. There's little chance that they'll use the program twice. There are few occupations more soul destroying than spending your evenings finding out exactly how much money you've squandered this week and projecting how much your checking account will be overdrawn next week. Compared to that, programming in assembler sounds like fun.

MICROS

As we've mentioned (see **mainframes**), in the bad old days, the word *computer* meant one of those big machines only large companies could afford. They did things like send bills for $333,333 threatening you with legal action if you didn't pay or letters beginning, "Dear Mr. 15 Main Street, Great News! You, Mr. 15 Main Street, have been selected . . . "

These practices gave rise to a sort of frightened respect for computers. They were intimidating things with unfathomable workings, and their commands were to be obeyed. Two great misconceptions based on **techno-fear** arose:

(1) Computers never make mistakes.
(2) All mistakes can be blamed on computer error.

You, however, know better. The **micro** has arrived — indeed, the word *computer* now brings to most people's minds the image of a home or business microcomputer, the kind of machine you see on sale at Sears or Wards or sitting in the corners of friends' dens gathering dust. Hundreds of thousands of people are realizing, as they use a computer for themselves at home and business, what arbitrary things they are. Technofear and even techno-reverence are now out, and anyone professing to know anything about computers should badmouth them all the time, saying that

(1) Computers make plenty of mistakes.
(2) All mistakes are caused by human error.

The line to take is "When you use one of the damn things for yourself, you realize how stupid they are." Invent ridiculous things which your, or your friend's, micro does, such as erase all data on the disk whenever you accidentally press the space bar and *M* together; or create a spurious document called *ABCDEFGH.doc* containing nothing but a stream of letter *F*s when you choose the "set tab stops" option on your word processor.

The reason computers keep making mistakes is

(1) the programs they run have been badly written
(2) the wires in the back have been badly soldered
(3) the user is asking the computer to do something silly, like sending a letter to all the names and addresses appearing in a grocery list instead of the address book
(4) "human error"

Human error is a term used by the writers of aircraft automatic-pilot programs to explain the crash. In technical terms it actually means "I thought the program would work, but I was wrong."

So, when those trying to impress you say they have computerized their small business with a micro, just laugh.

Which Micro?

People will tell you enthusiastically at parties which kind of machine they have, and if you know the main good and bad points of the most popular ones, you can either flatter their devotees for their wise choice or make them feel they've wasted their money.

Be careful in this area. Computer owners are very loyal to the brand of computer they've purchased and will defend their choice in much the same way that a mother bear will defend her cubs. No one will ever admit to buying a lemon, and the owner of brand X will harangue the owner of brand Z for hours in a futile attempt to convince him that X is the best machine. Brand loyalty in computers has replaced the "my football team is better than yours" or "my car outclasses yours" syndrome. BBFs spend hour upon hour on BBSs bashing the machines of brands other than their own. Indeed, most BBSs are machine specific, that is, they cater to BBFs of specific companies. There are IBM boards, Apple boards, Macintosh boards, Amiga boards, Commodore boards, and yes, even Atari boards. Most computers have their own magazines devoted to them, the number of which is directly proportional to the popularity, not necessarily the superiority, of that particular computer at that particular time.

IBM

When most people think of computers, they invariably think of **IBM,** one of the original TLA companies. IBM has dominated the computer field for so long that its name is synonymous with the word *computer* much the same as *Kleenex* has become the generic word for *tissues*. IBM is the world's biggest seller of computers, from the gigantic mainframes of big business, to the minicomputers of medium business, to the microcomputers of small business and personal use.

The IBM **PC** (**Personal Computer**) quickly established itself as the standard for home and business for no good reason other than that it had become the standard by which others were judged. Other companies brought out **clones,** (machines identical in every respect except the price, which was much lower). You should, therefore, never admit to having an IBM. IBM makes everything optional, including the keyboard, without which it is clearly impossible to operate the machine. It is rumored that in IBM's employee lunchrooms, lunch is only $2.00 — plus a dollar each for the optional knife, fork, and spoon.

So if anyone tells you they have a PC, you can say, "Oh, an IBM clone?" and they will probably agree, if only out of embarrassment. The company making the clone is immaterial. They are good general-purpose machines, although the technology they employ is quickly becoming outdated. Based on the PC's success, IBM introduced the **PC Jr.,** which was a disaster both technically and financially. The machines were said by some to be best used as doorstops or small boat anchors. The original PC was followed by IBM's **XT,** a faster and more powerful machine, and subsequently by the **AT,** an even faster and more powerful machine. When IBM recently introduced their "286" and "386" technology machines, many of the clone makers said enough is enough and banded together to keep the old IBM technology from being made obselete by IBM itself.

Always challenge someone who has a PC to tell you if it's an 8- or 16-bit machine. Whichever they say, suggest that it should be the other one. So, if you find someone who owns a 16-bit PC, say, "Ah yes, but it has only an 8-bit data bus." If they have an 8-bit PC, say, "Well, it's got 16-bit registers, of course."

A key to whether someone has a "real" IBM or a clone is the usage of the term **PC-DOS**. IBMers have PC-DOS, while cloners use **MS-DOS**. No difference really, just enough to keep the cloners out of court for plagiarism.

Good point. Nearly every program that has ever been written comes out in a form you can use on the PC, so you have the choice of all the best programs for everything.

Bad point. PCs are extremely boring and are essentially business machines. Only after a glut of uninteresting business software was produced did games start coming out for the PC, so you can hint that all PC owners are frustrated game players. This will annoy the non-game players, who will feel their intelligence is insulted, and the game players for having been unmasked.

Commodore and Apple

We'll take **Commodore** and **Apple** together, since they're basically almost identical except in appearance. These companies led the way to the introduction of microcomputers to the public in 1978. Commodore gave us the **PET 2001,** while Apple introduced what was to become a string of models that today are the most common computers found in schools. Commodore followed its PET with the **VIC-20,** the first computer truly built for playing games, and subsequently the **Commodore 64,** which may well turn out to be the number one computer in overall sales in the world.

All were 8-bit machines based on the **6502 microchip** and were relatively inexpensive game machines. For only a few months of mowing lawns and delivering newspapers, any teenager could afford one, complete with 20 varieties of space-invader games. Some ran programs from cassette and were incredibly slow and low tech, but nobody cared.

Good point. Just your basic, no-nonsense, unpretentious kind of computer that no one would be ashamed to start on.

Bad point. Just your basic, no-nonsense, unpretentious kind of computer that no one would admit to using now.

Amiga

The Amiga, produced by Commodore, is a 16-bit machine best known for its incredible graphics and ability to multitask. For computerists, multitasking is the ultimate capability. It allows the user to do two things at once (akin to walking and chewing gum at the same time), which ought to be easy but for many computers isn't. While the computer is printing out the first ten chapters of the owner's next best-selling book, he can be using his word processor to compose the following ten chapters, and all this time, his **spreadsheet** is calculating the vast profits he anticipates. All this presupposes the owner's ability to get all these programs up and running at the same time without **guruing** (**crashing** the machine). For the most practical purpose, you could use your Amiga at work to play games, immediately switching into your company's **database** when the boss walks in on you.

The Amiga is capable of producing 4096 colors on the screen at the same time, although one can only speculate on why anyone would need 4096 colors on the screen at the same time. Amigas are most often used by professional graphics artists, serious musicians, and serious game players. While early models were not compatible with the PC, the current A2000 series offers PC software compatibility. Theoretically, one can now have the best of all possible worlds, the ultimate in game machines and access to a wealth of business and applications software.

Good point. Incredible graphics and sound at a moderate price.

Bad point. Poor dealer support in many areas of the country.

Atari

Atari is Amiga's chief rival—a somewhat similar machine created, perhaps, in retaliation by the former president of Commodore. According to the gossips, Mr. T, having been ousted in a corporate battle, bought Atari and immediately laid plans for a challenger to the Amiga. This state of affairs has resulted in the longest rivalry since the Hatfields and the McCoys. Owners of both machines constantly proselytize, trying to convert one another to the preferred cult. If you find yourself in a room with both Amiga and Atari owners, you can increase the bloodletting by mentioning that the Amiga almost was an Atari product.

Good point. Very impressive graphics.

Bad point. Even less dealer support than for the Amiga.

Macintosh

The Macintosh is another product of the Apple Computer Corporation and probably the best known of the non-PC variety of machine. They are referred to as **Macs** and look like portable television sets. They are the machines of choice for graphics designers and desktop publishers. Early models had screens so small that it was like reading a newspaper using a telescope. Later models are much improved.

Good point. Very powerful software for graphics and desktop publishing is available, and the machine rivals the IBM in the small-business workplace.

Bad point. The computer, its peripherals, and its software are very expensive. No color (except for the Mac II, which is almost as expensive as a compact car).

Technical Questions

Your *detailed* knowledge of computers may lead someone to ask you a technical question. Never be worried about this; the fact that people ask means that they wouldn't understand the answer anyway. The most important rule is **claim to know nothing about the insides of machines.** Computer users should know no more about what happens behind the screen than a television critic does. If someone starts talking about *chips* and *processors* and *bus boards,* direct them to an electronic engineer (someone who says, "Four years ago I couldn't even spell engineer; now I are one").

Questions you will be asked are of three types:

(1) "Is there any way I can print sideways on my word processor?"

(2) "I'm running DBase V Version 2 under MS-DOS V3.0, and there seems to be a glitch at 34F5A938 which resets the defaults by overwriting four bytes at 8C60 when I run a batch file. Is there a kludge for this?"

(3) "My computer won't work; what's wrong with it?"

Adopt the old technique used by auto mechanics when customers ask them awkward questions.

(1) First ask them if they're using **Phoenix Bios**; if they say they are, comment with regret that you know nothing about Phoenix Bios. If they have some other system, say you know about nothing *but* Phoenix Bios. But generously offer to listen to their question anyway.

(2) Listen intently and ask what version of the program they're talking about; then say, "Oh, that version; there were problems with that one."

(3) Go deep into thought for a few seconds; then pick the most suitable of the following answers:

— "Yes, you can do it, but it's very difficult unless you know assembler." (Nobody asking a question of you will know assembler, so no problem here.)

— "There's a program in the public domain that will do it for you with a little tweaking. I've forgotten the name, but it's something like V-G8HG.EXE." (This is always true.)

— "I think there's a bug on that version that's been fixed in the latest version." (All versions of all programs have bugs, which get fixed in the next version, which reveals further bugs, so you're safe here too.)

Remember, those asking questions want only your time, not your advice. If they really wanted to find out how to do something, they would go to a computer consultant and pay $50 an hour; in talking to you, they think they are getting attention free. They will therefore be unimpressed by a short reply which answers the question perfectly and succinctly. They will, on the other hand, be pathetically grateful for ten minutes of your scratching your head, ooing and ahing and ending up saying, "You can do it, but it's very difficult unless you know assembler."

APPLICATIONS

Applications is just another word for *programs,* although it sounds better. The question is, once you've bought a computer, what do you use it for? More important, what should you be telling people to use *theirs* for instead of wasting their time doing what they're doing with it now?

Everyone knows that computers are powerful tools and that they can do lots of things. Few people know *what.* The idea is to sound as though *you* know what they should be doing to get more out of their machine. Find out, therefore, what their present major use is and tell them the disadvantages (listed below), suggesting that they really should be doing something else. It doesn't matter what model they have; the following applies to any home or business microcomputer.

Note that the name of any program with pretentions has spurious capitals in the middle of the name — *MegaBase, WonderCalc,* and so forth.

Word Processors

Instead of typing out your documents on a clanky old typewriter, the point of **word processors** is that you type the documents into your computer, which stores the text on disk. You can then edit pieces of the text, format it as you like, reset the line spacing, move chunks of text around, etc., as you wish. All these things take place instantly on the screen, and you print out the document only when you're satisfied that it's perfect.

Typical programs. *WordStar, WordPerfect, ProWrite, word* or *write* plus anything.

Disadvantages. Documents fall into two types:

(1) quick letters and memos
(2) longer documents where presentation is all important, such as business reports and newsletters

For the letters and memos, it's clearly more trouble than it's worth to turn on your computer, load the operating system, boot up the word processor, type in your letter, check it, print it out, print it out again because the first one was too far to the left in the printer, save it to disk, and turn the computer off. "What you need," you say, "is a good old fashioned electric typewriter, which will do the job much quicker."

For the longer documents, word processors are usually not powerful enough to cope with the functions you need – two-column printing, footnotes, graphs and illustrations, etc. "What you really should be using," you tell them, "is a desktop publisher."

Desktop Publishers

Desktop publishers let you manipulate text into columns, make up graphics in boxes, and then place it all on a page to get the best arrangement before printing it out. Used for newsletters, posters, fliers, and so forth.

Typical programs. *PageMaker, PrintMaster, PageSetter, Publisher Plus, page* or *print* plus anything.

Disadvantages. Desktop publishers fail on two counts – they neither have the quality of output you can get from traditional typesetting-plus-pasteup to make them good for "real" newsletters and posters nor are they quick and easy enough to use to make them worthwhile for simple purposes.

"What you really want," you say, "is a word processor – then get your word-processed text typeset, pasted up, and printed with the graphics and photos professionally prepared. It looks so much better."

Graphics Packages and CAD Programs

Graphics and **CAD (Computer Assisted Design)** are the software equivalent of a drawing board or an artist's easel. You can do things like drawing technical and freehand graphics, painting pictures using an almost unlimited palette of colors, storing them on disk, editing them, and printing them out.

Typical programs. *DeluxePaint, DrawPlus, AutoCAD, paint, draw,* or *CAD* plus anything.

Disadvantages. These programs usually have lousy facilities for handling text or captions to describe your drawings. "So much better," you say, "to have a desktop publisher which has good graphics capabilities – you can then caption and annotate your drawings to your heart's content."

Desktop Video

Desktop video is a relatively new area of specialization—useful for creating animations and adding screen titles to home movies you've created with your **video camera** or **camcorder.**

Typical programs. *DeluxeVideo, ProVideo,* or *video* plus anything.

Disadvantages. Using these programs effectively presupposes that you either own a television station or at least have the financial means of buying one should you desire. Programs are extremely expensive, but nothing compared to what you'll spend for the rest of the equipment. "Better to invest in a graphics or paint program," you suggest, "create a bunch of cartoon drawings, and shuffle through them quickly to simulate real motion. Take your home videos to a video store, and let them superimpose the titles on your creations."

Financial Packages

Financial programs record the incomings and outgoings of all of your funds and let you know in the wink of an eye how you stand financially. That's about the most interesting thing that can be said about home or business finance packages. Some will let you do your income taxes at home, but the guilt of putting millions of H&R Block employees on welfare will probably keep you up at night.

Typical programs. *Your Home Finances* or *money* or *tax* plus anything.

Disadvantages, It's been said that the absolutely worst reason in the world for purchasing a home computer is to "balance your checkbook," which is probably the world's biggest understatement. People who would spend six hours per month using a computer to keep track of their checking account would be much wiser spending their money for psychiatric therapy. "What you really need here," you comment, "is a spreadsheet, where you can design your financial recordkeeping requirements to your own needs."

Spreadsheets

"**Spreadsheets** have been around for only ten years or so, but the concept of a database goes back to the U.S. census of 1890," you say confidently. Spreadsheets replace the back of an envelope for making calculations. You define structures, for example, making the total at the foot of a column equal to the sum of all the numbers in that column, and then see what happens if you change one of the numbers somewhere in the structure. Great for making "what-if" calculations.

Typical programs. *Lotus 1-2-3* or anything ending in *-Calc.*

Disadvantages. Spreadsheets have thousands of uses, "limited only by your imagination." Unfortunately, no one can ever imagine what to use their spreadsheets for or how to make them do something once they've thought of it. Tell your avid listener, "It's always best to buy a program for the specific use you have in mind; a personal finance program, for example."

Databases

Databases handle information – typically the name-and-address-plus-details lists for businesses and clubs. You can select certain groups, sort all your entries into order of name or amount owed to you, print them out, and so forth. The word also means a store of information as well as the program that handles it.

Typical programs. *Dbase III* or anything ending in *-Base*

Disadvantages. You hardly ever do anything important with a database, except keep lists of people to whom you send letters when something happens – when they owe you money or their subscriptions run out. "Instead of bothering with setting up complicated databases, it's much easier," you assert, "to buy a mail list program and deal with the letter sending directly."

Mail List Programs

Mail list programs are those which take a name-and-address file on the one hand and a letter with areas marked out on the other and fill the areas appropriately with information from the address file, making a letter for each name. You can vary the contents of the letter according to information in the name-and-address file. These are the programs that send you letters beginning with, "Dear Mr. Johnx5on – Great news! You, Mr. Johnx5on, have been selected from all the people in New Jersey to take part in our prize drawing . . . "

Typical programs. Anything with *-Mail* or *-Merge.*

Disadvantages. You always screw things up, and after printing 15,000 letters to your customers, you realize they read, "Dear. Mr. 15 High St, You have been selected from all our customers in East Dwiddle to receive ... " "What you really need," you insist, "is something which helps and *knows* not to put the wrong thing in the wrong place – say, a database."

Games

  Games of old were very basic. All you had were little green blobs who were about to invade the earth, and the only way to communicate with them was to shoot them down. Now, with more and more sophisticated technology, you have all the colors and shapes of aliens in 3-D, who can play chess with you as they invade – but all you can still do is shoot them down.

Typical games. Any game is typical.

Disadvantages. There are so many games around that any given game will have several dozen look-alikes, some of which will be better but most of which nobody will ever have heard of. So you can make up any name you like, and no one will be able to disagree with you. For example, when someone says how good this game they just bought is, *Zappa-Noid,* you just smile and say

  (1) "That's just a *Klarch* clone, isn't it?"
  (2) "*Space Sniper* has more levels."
  (3) "*Mutants of Warp Zone III* has better graphics."
  (4) "The version for Atari is useless" (or "better," depending on which computer they have.)

Viruses

A **virus** is a hidden program which gets into the system of your machine from copied (read **pirated**) software or public domain programs. It copies itself to your floppies or your hard disk—and after it has reproduced itself a few times, it either wipes out the disk on which it has attached itself or just announces to you via a screen message that it could have wiped out the disk should the originator have chosen to do so. By this time, it's already on many of your other disks, and if you've loaned disks to others, all of theirs as well.

Viruses are usually the products of either sick minds or disgruntled employees of software companies who have been fired and are seeking revenge. Virus-checking and removing programs which can cope with most of the more infectious types are now proliferating. The phenomenon is quite serious, as the consequences for, say, a hospital or military establishment would be disastrous.

The bluffer has nothing to fear. If you never use a computer, you cannot be affected by a virus. You can, however, worry everyone you meet. When they tell you what computer they own, roll your eyes and say, "Oh oh, they've just discovered a deadly, undetectable virus on that one . . . " If you back away from the person as you say this, it will be even more effective.

LANGUAGES

BASIC

You can write programs to do just about anything, which is strange because all programming enthusiasts ever do is talk about writing routines to calculate primes and argue about whether the Shell sort to put names into alphabetical order is faster in *C* or *Modula-2*.

You can write such programs in a variety of different computer **languages.** Remember two easy rules:

(1) The easiest to write produce the slowest running programs.

(2) The most difficult yield the fastest.

Professional programmers talk about complex languages such as **BASIC** (in which the command to print a character to the screen might be something very simple like "PRINT A$") and simple languages like **assembler** (in which the same command might take up 20 lines of nonsense like "PUSH A," "SHLD LX1," "HD(HX)87," and so forth). The assembler version works far faster, of course – by as much as several dozen milliseconds.

The only viewpoint you can have is that BASIC, despite being frowned upon by "real" programmers, is fine for doing anything, and writing in assembler is an unnecessary waste of time. Denounce anyone who claims that writing in assembler is easy as stark raving mad.

Arguments for using BASIC are

(1) It's easy to learn.
(2) It's easy to use.
(3) It can do all the other languages can do and more.
(4) Its slowness is negligible if used on a fast computer.
(5) Most important, it annoys computer freaks and hackers immensely to have someone refusing to put BASIC down.

Sooner or later you'll have to explain to someone what the difference is between a **compiled** language, like **C**, and an **interpreted** language, like BASIC. Put on your best I'll-put-it-in-man-in-the-street-terms voice, and explain how a compiled language is like a professionally done translation and an interpreted language is like a phrase book. The latter is translated line by line into machine code, and as in a phrase book, conversation can be verbose, tautological, and clumsy. The former is more efficient and elegant and won't say things twice, but clearly the phrase book version is easiest for conversation. Indeed, developing a program which involves "talking" to your computer is best done with an interpreted language like BASIC.

BASIC stands for **Beginners All-Purpose Symbolic Instruction Code,** a fact you need to remember only for bar bets. It's the language everyone starts on, but those who "move on" to other languages regard it as a stage they've gone through and look down on it. Defend it fiercely with such points as

(1) "Come on, program development is so much more convenient with an interpreted language."

(2) "But BASIC is so easy; you can concentrate on the program instead of trying to remember the syntax of your language."

(3) "I'm sorry, with 16- and 32-bit machines available, I don't see why we should have to spend months writing a five-line BASIC listing in assembler to gain a few more milliseconds of speed."

Other languages, you should imply, are an unnecessarily complex and pedantic way of doing what sound, common-sense, practical people like yourself can do in BASIC much more quickly ("It may not be elegant, but it does the job").

Others

There are plenty of other languages available, and if you stick to your BASIC-is-good-enough-for-practical-purposes guns, you need know only enough about the other main languages to dismiss them out of hand.

Know about **generations**.

First-generation languages are raw and work at a simple level on the machine, so they are incredibly tedious to program with. (Machine code is first generation: a program in machine code would read like 01001011 10010100 00010010 10001001, etc.).

Second-generation is assembler.

Third-generation languages include more sensible ones, like BASIC, which have almost comprehensible instructions like PRINT TOTAL, STOP, TAX=COST × TAXRATE, etc.

Fourth-generation languages will write a third-generation program, so you can effectively give one command like "write me a program to total up these numbers and calculate the tax on them," and it will do just that.

Nobody really understands **fifth-generation languages,** so you can say anything you like about them so long as it includes the phrase "artificial intelligence" a lot.

Here, then, is a partial list of languages.

Ada

Ada is sometimes known as the "military language" due to its use as the "official" language of both the U.S. Department of Defense and the U.K. Ministry of Defense. Like anything associated with the military, this one is equally as confusing to those who know the language as to those who don't.

Dismissal. "But it's only a third-generation language."

Assembler

Assembler is also known as "machine language" because only a machine can understand it.

Dismissal. "But writing in assembler is so boring and such a complete waste of time."

C

C is the new defacto standard for programmers. Very big in universities.

Dismissal. "It looks like Martian. How can you ever understand a program someone else has written?"

Forth

Forth is a threaded language with roots in astronomy.

Dismissal. "Forth? Hah! Great for moving telescopes and calculating azimuthal angles, I suppose."

LOGO

LOGO was developed in California for teaching kids programming skills. It uses a "turtle" to draw little graphics patterns recursively.

Modula-2

A relative newcomer to the computer language arts, **Modula-2**'s name would indicate that there was a Modula-1, but no one has ever heard of it.

Dismissal. "Well I suppose Mod-2 is all right if you're not bright enough to learn C."

Pascal

Pascal is a standard teaching language which forces you into developing good programming habits.

Dismissal. "Great teaching language, but no file handling – obviously academics never thought you'd actually want to use it for anything."

Prolog

Prolog is an artificial intelligence programming language.

Dismissal. "Well of course, Prolog's very interesting, I suppose . . . "

Others

LISP, Talk, SmallTalk, Fortran (the math language that almost no one speaks anymore), COBOL (formerly the language of business—replaced by C), True BASIC, FBASIC, TinyBASIC, and on and on and on . . .

HISTORY

Knowledge of the history of computers is essential. The first point to make is that computing is not just decades old, as people think, but "has been around for centuries." The belief that computers did not exist before 1950 is perpetuated mainly by BBFs. They do not recognize machines before then because there weren't enough computers in the world to make it worthwhile communicating with them.

Origins

Claim that the Greeks (always a safe bet—they invented most things) were the first to invent computing methods—**Erastosthenes**, for example, invented a computer-program-like way of finding prime numbers. Realizing that if they did have computers, people would then do nothing but waste their time working out endless lists of prime numbers, the Greeks wisely desisted from inventing one.

The first real calculating machine was the **abacus**, in use in ancient China thousands of years ago. It's still used in many places in the Orient today, such as Japan, usually to check the work of fifth-generation computers. At this point, someone usually jumps up and claims that skilled abacus users can add up a column of figures faster than a calculator can—say four seconds for a calculator but three for an abacus. Always say that this is nonsense, since it disregards the three years spent learning how to use an abacus, making the time to add a column of figures three years and three seconds.

Calculating

The mechanization of calculation was left to Scotsman **John Napier,** who discovered **logarithms** around the turn of the 1600s. Logarithms proved to be the key to multiplication and division, a feat at which the abacus is dismally deficient, and also to the invention of the slide rule to do these operations quickly and easily.

Napier is therefore a key figure for the bluffer to remember, partly because his contribution was important but mainly because the words *logarithm* and *slide rule* (and *Scotsman*) intimidate people, keep them from asking awkward questions, and make you sound confident and wise.

Blaise Pascal, son of a French tax collector, made the next step in 1642. He built a calculating machine to help his father do his taxes and is therefore another good name to remember for the same reason as Napier.

This machine could still only add and subtract, mainly subtract, in fact, given its original purpose, and it was **Leibnitz** thirty years later who developed the calculating machine idea into the form used right up to the 1940s. It wasn't until the 1970s that British entrepreneur **Clive Sinclair** pioneered the electronic calculator. You must claim to have owned one of the first when they came out and say that they cost $75, were the size of a hardback book, and could only add, subtract, multiply, and divide "but were amazing at the time."

Real Computers

Calculation is only one facet of computing, although granted a very *useful* (boring) one. The real definition of a computer is something which can be programmed to do different things, such as work out prime numbers and other more *interesting* (completely useless and timewasting) tasks.

The breakthrough in programmable machines was a loom invented by **Joseph Jacquard** in 1805 which could weave different patterns according to which cards were fed into its controller. A pattern could be coded into a set of cards, just like a program. Unfortunately, the weavers at Lyon were upset by the unemployment prospects and tried to drown him in the Rhone. You can try using this fact as a clinching point in an argument for or against new technology in the workplace.

Britisher **Charles Babbage** is the major figure in the history of computers (even today having a chain of computer stores named after him). Bluffers should know that he not only left his brain to the Royal College of Surgeons, but also developed two **proto-computers** (a good phrase to use) in the mid 1800s, the *Difference Engine* and the more ambitious *Analytical Engine*. The first set many patterns for R and D (research and development): it was decades ahead of its time (having punch-card input and printed output, for example), and it was abandoned before completion because of a lack of money, although a model was later built in Sweden. The second **engine** set even greater standards for R and D — it was never built at all.

The thing to remember is that the punch cards were prepared by **Ada,** Lord Byron's daughter, who was therefore the world's first computer programmer and who set the pattern for programmers-to-come by becoming hooked on drink and drugs.

Technology then bridged the Atlantic to do the U.S. census of 1890. This event was the real birth of **data processing** — the concept of using machines to process *vital* (incredibly boring and repetitive) information. Faced with the prospect of the census results taking so long to process that they would not be ready until after the next census had been taken, the government brought in **Herman Hollerith,** who put all the information on punch cards and processed the whole batch in two and a half years.

Hollerith realized that there was a market for processing incredibly boring information for businesses and started a company; in 1911 it became IBM, which the acid-tongued have suggested has such a high employee turnover that they have to keep developing new computers just to keep track of their personnel records.

The War

It wasn't until World War II that technology had developed to the point where the ideas on computer design that went back to Babbage could be put into practice. The war is a rewarding area to profess knowledge about because

(1) A lot of significant developments occurred.

(2) Much more important, information about the R and D is still classified, so you can say whatever you want and no one can call you on it.

To break the Germans' "Enigma" codes, the British mathematician **Alan Turing** organized the building of the **Colossus,** a huge machine containing 1500 tubes. It cracked the codes, and even by today's standards, it wasn't bad — it could probably decipher the conversation between two modern-day BBFs.

After the war, the technicians who had been working on war computers carried out their research for more peaceful purposes. Most of them spent their time thinking up acronymic names for their computers, such as ENIAC, EDSAC, EDVAC, UNIVAC, and ACE. The only important thing to remember about these scientists is that they were all great for mathematical calculations but couldn't do anything at all like remembering their mothers' telephone numbers, and it was the same for the computers they designed. The computers were larger though, about the size of a studio apartment in New York, and even more expensive.

Business

At this point, IBM began to dominate the world of business computing — probably because IBM gave their computers uninteresting names, like 701 and 1401, and so appealed to businessmen.

Technology

From the late 50s to the present day has been one

long march of progress and developing technology. **Transistors** were the first major breakthrough and meant not only that computers were smaller, but also that operators could listen to pocket radios as they worked. Punch cards were replaced by **magnetic tape**, meaning that operators could then listen to their favorite groups on cassettes as well. The huge reels of magnetic tape were replaced by small **disks,** meaning you could now ruin an entire disk by spilling a single cup of coffee, whereas before you could ruin only a couple of inches of tape.

The IBM 360 in 1965 was the first really cost-effective business computer. Every business bought one, which meant they were committed to IBM systems. You should note that this ensured IBM's domination of the business market ever since, despite being, according to some, neither the best nor the cheapest.

The advent of **microprocessors,** in which many thousands of transisters could be put on a chip of **silicon,** spawned the growth of the **microcomputer** industry in the late 70s and early 80s. Until then, computers had been huge things in the basement of the Pentagon with large reels of tape, easily sabotaged by international gangs of terrorists disguised in white coats who would start World War III. With the benefits of new technology, however, computers became small, television-sized machines which pimple-faced adolescents could use to hack into the Pentagon's defense system and start World War III.

As for future technology, the vital names to drop are

(1) **RISC** technology, which means even more things can be put on a silicon chip (you don't have to

remember what RISC means; just make derogatory remarks about it).

(2) **Transputers,** which have the remarkable property that ten of them linked together are ten times as powerful as one.

It's always good to mention the story of the episode on *Star Trek* in which Spock and Kirk come back to earth of the 1960s. Finding a big old reel-to-reel computer, it takes them a few seconds to recognize it. "Look," they say, "a primitive computer." You can note smugly that we can now agree with them.

GLOSSARY

Address—Where a byte lives in memory. Always expressed as combinations like C84A or B20E.

BBF—Bulletin Board (see *BBS*) Freak. A computer owner who spends countless hours using a *modem* and a telephone to connect to *message centers* where he reads messages left by others, retrives programs left there for free distribution, and if really lucky, communicates with the SYSOP (system operator) or another computer owner.

BBS—Bulletin Board System. A computer connected to a telephone by modem (see *Modem*) to allow computer owners to leave messages and get free programs. Access is usually free unless the SYSOP is feeling less than philanthropic.

Blitter Chip—The part of a computer which handles the moving of objects around the screen, giving computer magazines endless puns (the blitter end, blitter sweet, etc).

Bug—Mistake in a program, occasionally called *feature* by the author of the program ("a feature of *MegaBase* is that pressing SHIFT-CONTROL-Q will erase all of the files on the disk").

Byte—Just enough space for one letter, or number below 256. "Just a bit of information," except, of course, that a byte is really 8 bits.

CAD – Computer Assisted Design. The idea of doing technical drawings on a computer instead of on a piece of paper. Also stands for *Crude and Disappointing*.

Crash – To stop working irretrievably. The only usual remedy is to switch off the power, switch it back on, and start again. Also what some programmers have been known to do after having spent 39 consecutive hours drinking Coke and playing *Marble Madness*.

Data – Information, but easier for writers of manuals to spell.

Endless Loop – See *Infinite Loop*.

Environment – Meaningless add-on word. Talk about *MS-DOS* but more impressively *MS-DOS environment*. Similarly *WIMP environment*, *WordStar environment*, *crash environment*, etc.

File – Any single thing stored on a disk: a program, some sort of data for a program (maybe records about your stock of nails, which would be a nail file), or a text document like a recipe (in which case you'd be putting a cake in a file).

Hardware – The difference between hardware (equipment) and software (programs) is this. Hardware starts off working OK, but more and more things go wrong the older it gets (like people); software starts off full of bugs, but more and more of them get fixed the older it gets.

Icon – Representation of something on screen by a picture instead of words, possibly as a result of game players' dubious literacy.

Infinite Loop – See *Endless Loop*.

Joystick – Device used to operate games. Loved by computer magazines for the headline "The Joy of Sticks."

K – Kilobyte. Measurement of space on a disk (either floppy or hard). In computerese this represents 1024 bytes, from the Greek *kilo* meaning *1000*, because nobody knew what "1024" was in Greek.

Meg – Short for *megabyte*. One thousand *k*, or is it 1024k (1,024,000 bytes, or maybe 1024×1024=1,048,576, or perhaps just 1,000,000. Not even *War and Peace* was as big as a megabyte. (1,048,576 bytes is correct).

Menu – List of options you have at a point in a program just like a restaurant menu – everything has a misleading name, and whatever you want is never available.

Modem – Device enabling your computer to link up to another computer via the telephone at great expense and do things from your living room, like pay your phone bill.

Mouse – Hand-size box with several buttons, which runs on a ball and moves the cursor on the screen – by clicking the mouse button you can activate the thing pointed to. Make people believe it is an acronym for *Manually Operated Utility Selection Equipment*. It isn't. Computer designers really think *mice* look like mice. They don't. You can spot truly round-the-bend computer freaks if they have a cloth cover for the mouse when it's not in use. A mousepad is essential however, else your mouse would skid all over your desk. Don't worry about your cat eating your "mouse." If it does, you have made a grave error in giving it food and lodging all these years.

Recursion – See *Recursion*.

Technical Support – What your computer store promises you'll get if you buy from them. So-called free advice on how to use the program. *So-called* because, when you call, the line is always busy or the company has gone bankrupt.

RAM – Wherever you are, you should remember that this is *Random Access Memory*.

Rem – A line put into a program which is not an instruction comprehensible to the computer. It is a remark equally incomprehensible to the programmer who wrote it when he looks at the program to debug it four months later.

ROM – *Read Only Memory*. Two ROMs don't make a write.

SCSI – Pronounced *scuzzy* and standing for *Small Computer System Interface*. One of the favorite after-dinner topics of Macintosh users – "My SCSI drive crashed due to a ROM bug in the new DOS."

Upgrade – Improved version of a program with the old bugs taken out and new ones put in.

WIMP – System using a mouse, as in *Windows, Icons, Mouse, and Pointers,* but more likely a reference to those too afraid of using the keyboard to type in commands.